CASTLE-BUILDING IN THIRTEENTH-CENTURY WALES AND SAVOY

BY

A. J. TAYLOR

ALBERT RECKITT
ARCHAEOLOGICAL LECTURE
BRITISH ACADEMY
1977

FROM THE PROCEEDINGS OF THE
BRITISH ACADEMY, LONDON, VOLUME LXIII (1977)
OXFORD UNIVERSITY PRESS

ISBN 0 85672 160 3

Printed in Great Britain
at the University Press, Oxford
by Eric Buckley
Printer to the University

CASTLE-BUILDING IN THIRTEENTH-CENTURY WALES AND SAVOY

By A. J. TAYLOR

Fellow of the Academy

Read 23 November 1977

ON this Wednesday thirty-three years ago our much lamented Fellow the late Sir Goronwy Edwards delivered to the Academy his Sir John Rhŷs Memorial Lecture on the subject of 'Edward I's Castle-building in Wales'.[1] In a characteristically penetrating and lucid paper he examined and set before us, in a way unlikely to be superseded, the documentary evidence preserved in the Public Record Office for the creation of eight new royal castles: Builth, only its Norman earthworks now rising beside the Wye; Aberystwyth, war- and weather-worn since the time of Glyndŵr; Flint and Rhuddlan; Conway and Harlech; Caernarvon and Beaumaris. These were all castles which King Edward began, and in all but two cases completed, in mid and North Wales between 1277 and 1295. The study broke new ground in that it was the first time the building of these great works had been considered as a single state enterprise, costing so much money, requiring the recruitment and movement of so much labour, calling for special expedients of finance, and taking this or that number of years to carry through. It will not be unknown to some of you here this evening that I have myself been moved to devote a good deal of time to pursuing one aspect which Sir Goronwy specifically excluded, namely the architecture of the castles, and in particular its authorship and affinities. Though many of my findings have already been published over the years,[2] I think the time has perhaps come for me to give some account of the investigations that led to them.

---

[1] *Proceedings of the British Academy*, xxxii (1953), 15–81.

[2] 'Master James of St. George', *English Historical Review*, lxv (1950), 433–57; 'The Date of Caernarvon Castle', *Antiquity*, xxvi (1952), 25–34; 'A letter from Lewis of Savoy to Edward I', *English Historical Review*, lxviii (1953), 55–62; 'The Castle of St. Georges-d'Epéranche', *Antiquaries Journal*, xxxiii (1953), 33–47; 'Castle-building in Wales in the Later Thirteenth Century:

I make no apology for doing so within the ambit of an archaeological lecture, for to observe and study the architectural
minutiae of medieval constructions is often to elucidate their
archaeology. One of the purposes of the Trust under whose
auspices this lecture is given is defined as the encouragement of
'the exploration of ancient sites in any part of the world . . . and
the publication of the results thereof', and provided ancient
sites may be construed as including medieval castles I think I
may claim my subject falls within the terms of reference. Indeed,
what I am now going to place before you is the account of how
one such exploration was carried on and correlated not in one
part of the world only, but in two parts simultaneously, over a
period of more than twenty years. In both the regions concerned
it has been an exploration not only of buildings but also of
records, so that a sub-title of the paper might have added the
words 'in the light of field-work and archives'. At all events I
take my cue from Sir Mortimer Wheeler's light-hearted description of the Reckitt Fund as one whose mild restrictions
'have enabled it to be used profitably over a wide range of
projects in which "research" and "discovery" are not too
narrowly defined and discriminated'.[1]

It has been said that what historians seek is affected by what
they see.[2] I do not claim any special perceptiveness but I
certainly enjoyed unusual opportunities. As Inspector of
Ancient Monuments for Wales from 1946 to 1955 I had the
chance to become totally familiar with the North Wales castles,
to notice things that were like and things that were unlike, to
compare resemblances of detail, checking the treatment of this
or that feature in one building against its corresponding treatment in another, looking if need be at three or four castles in the
course of a single summer day for the repetition or absence of

the Prelude to Construction', in *Studies in Building History: essays in recognition
of the work of B. H. St. J. O'Neil*, ed. E. M. Jope (London, 1961), 104–33;
'Some Notes on the Savoyards in North Wales, 1277–1300, with special
reference to the Savoyard element in the construction of Harlech Castle',
Genava, N.S. tome XI (Genève, 1963) (Mélanges d'histoire et d'archéologie
offerts en hommage à M. Louis Blondel), 289–315; 'The King's Works in
Wales, 1277–1330', in *The History of the King's Works*, ed. H. M. Colvin
(London, 1963), i. 293–408, ii. 1027–40; 'The Walls of Conway', *Archaeologia
Cambrensis*, cxix (1970), 1–9; 'Who was "John Pennardd, leader of the men of
Gwynedd"?', *English Historical Review*, xc (1976), 79–97.

[1] Mortimer Wheeler, *The British Academy 1949–1968* (London, 1970), 52–3.

[2] Margaret Aston, 'English Ruins and English History: The Dissolution
and the Sense of the Past', *Journal of the Warburg and Courtauld Institutes*, xxxvi
(1973), 254.

some particular constructional quirk, and storing in memory or on film impressions for comparison elsewhere when occasion might arise. The familiarity thus gradually gained led me to identify five constructional or architectural features that were not to my knowledge paralleled in other English or Welsh castles and were therefore likely to be directly derived from a continental source. They were as follows:

1. First there is the use, in the construction of towers and curtain walls alike, of helicoidal or inclined scaffold paths up which materials could be hauled or winched as buildings advanced in height. Evidence of this is to be seen in the sloping lines of putlog holes which are prominent throughout the castles of Conway, Harlech, and Beaumaris and on the town walls of Conway and Caernarvon (Plates XXIII–XXIV). For an example reflecting the use of orthodox horizontal scaffolding one may contrast the long rows of putlog holes to be seen in the walls of the Bishop of Chichester's fourteenth-century castle at Amberley, Sussex.

2. Next there is the sporadic use of the full-centred semi-circular arch, over doors, gateways, embrasures, and windows. Examples are to be seen in embrasures at Flint, Conway, and Harlech; in the gatehouse at Harlech and in the great end window of the hall at Conway; in the barbican gate at Beaumaris; and high up over the Queen's Gate at Caernarvon (Plates XXVI–XXIX).

3. At Harlech there occur two distinctive types of garderobe construction. In the first the shaft is contained in a shallow projection occupying the angle of inner curtain and corner tower and extending almost the full height of the curtain wall; in the second we have a large half-round projection corbelled out from the outer curtain at courtyard level to overhang the rock-cut ditch below (Plate XXX).

4. A fourth feature is the embellishment of the crenellation of Conway castle with groups of three stone pinnacles or finials originally surmounting the cresting of every merlon. The same treatment was applied to the town walls, where today only one finial is left out of the hundreds there must have been originally (Plate XXXI).[1]

[1] Stumps of finials surviving on pieces of original cresting at Caernarvon castle, particularly on the Watch Tower and the curtain wall to the east of it, may indicate original decoration similar to Conway's, and not necessarily the repetition of the sculptured figures seen on the Eagle Tower.

5. Fifth and last, Harlech has a series of notably distinctive windows, lighting the four principal rooms of the castle gatehouse; nothing closely comparable to them appears to have survived elsewhere in this country. There are eight windows altogether, three facing west into the courtyard on each of the two main floor levels, and, on the topmost floor only, one in each of the short north and south end walls. The six westward-facing windows have at some time been severely modified, their tracery lights having been suppressed, their segmental heads lowered and reset at the level of the transoms, and the resulting space under the relieving arches filled up with blocks of ashlar. Only in the two end windows does the stone framing survive to its full original height, but between them these two retain enough fragments of their destroyed mullions, transoms, tracery, shutter fittings, and glazing grooves to allow accurate reconstruction of the original form of the whole group (Plate XXXII).

These, then, the helicoidal scaffold holes, the full-centred arches, the distinctive forms of certain garderobes, the triple finials at Conway, and the gatehouse windows at Harlech, stood out as five well-defined features whose area of origin seemed to be unknown and to deserve location and exploration. Moreover, if that area could be discovered, and its relationship established on a basis not merely of architectural resemblances, which can be deceptive, but of resemblances backed by documentation, which may be decisive, then the way might also be opened to the explanation of an unknown of even greater interest than the resemblances themselves: namely the problem, for such it then was, of the identity and previous whereabouts of the Master James of St. George who from at least 1285 onwards is referred to in our English records as the *magister operacionum Regis in Wallia*. As long ago as 1937 I had noted the earliest references to him as *Magister Jacobus Ingeniator*, or *Magister Jacobus Le Mazun* in the 1277–8 wardrobe book,[1] and as time went on I was led increasingly to believe that Master James probably had not, as such men as Robert of Beverley or Walter of Hereford presumably had, an English professional background.

It was with these two purposes in view, therefore, to search on the one hand for architectural parallels and on the other for authentic sources for dating them, which might also perhaps

[1] PRO, C47/4/1, fos. 11d, 16d, 22d, 34.

throw light on the overriding problem of authorship, that I set out from England in the autumn of 1950.[1] If one went with little hesitation to Savoy, this was only because there were many pointers in the direction of that historic princedom lying astride the Alpine passes, its thirteenth-century bounds embracing territories that are today partly in western Switzerland, partly in north-west Italy, partly in eastern France. First, was there not the close family relationship between King Edward I and Savoy's ruling Count Philip, whose sister Beatrice was the mother of Eleanor of Provence and grandmother of the king? Philip's more famous predecessor Peter of Savoy, to whom Henry III had given the honour of Richmond and lordship of Pevensey, and Archbishop Boniface of Canterbury were his brothers; his nephew Amadeus, later (1285–1323) Count Amadeus the Great, was with King Edward's army at Montgomery in the first Welsh war of 1277 and captain of the army of Chester at the beginning of the war of 1282.[2] It was from this family tie that there arose the remarkable arrangement under which succesive counts of Savoy actually held of, and did homage to the kings of England as their feudal overlords for, the castle of Avigliana within distant sight of Turin, the town of Susa, the palace and castle of Bard, beyond Aosta, today covered by a derelict Napoleonic fort, and the town of St. Maurice in Chablais with its watch-tower commanding a vital Rhône crossing, each of them a key point on one of the transalpine routes over the Mont Cenis or the Great St. Bernard.[3]

Furthermore one could hardly forget that Edward had chosen a Savoyard, his lifetime friend and confidant Sir Otto de Grandison, to be the first justiciar of North Wales under the settlement of 1284. Amongst many Savoyards brought by the

[1] The journey owed something of its inspiration to T. E. Lawrence, *Crusader Castles* (Golden Cockerel Press, 2 vols., 1936), a copy of which had been given me in 1949 by E. T. Leeds, sometime Keeper of the Ashmolean and a good friend to both Lawrence and the writer.

[2] For references to Amadeus in Wales, see *Eng. Hist. Rev.* lxviii. 56, n. 2. It is not unlikely that he was the writer of a letter addressed 'Au Roy de Engleterre' and sent on 3 April 1277 from the besieged Welsh castle of Dolforwyn near Montgomery (*Cal. Anc. Correspondence Wales*, ed. J. G. Edwards, 30–1). Its writer's expressed unwillingness to entrust the surrendered castle's repair to Master Bertram, who had by then already been thirty years in the king's service (cf. *Hist. King's Wks.* ii. 1036–7), may foreshadow the procurement of Master James of St. George from Savoy for Wales early in the following year.

[3] F. M. Powicke, *King Henry III and the lord Edward* (Oxford, 1947), i. 365, ii. 612–13 and n.

dynastic connection into the circle of the English royal household Otto was pre-eminent, and to Otto had been given, according to his biographer C. L. Kingsford, a special charge for the building and care of Edward's new castles.[1] Otto's own castle of Grandson (Plate XXXIV*c*)[2] beside the lake of Neuchâtel might indeed still be visited, as likewise could his tomb (Plate XXXIV*b*)[3] in the cathedral of Lausanne above Lac Léman. And again, the chief residence of the counts of Savoy used to be the island castle of Chillon, still standing intact on the margin of the Léman (Plate XXXIV*a*), and it was here that Amadeus, whose presence in Wales with King Edward we have already noticed, had been married in 1272.[4] I also retained a vivid picture of having twice seen from the train somewhere in this same region a ruined castle, afterwards identified as Saillon in the Valais, whose very stance and build had seemed to me even from a mile away to have an affinity of form and line with Conway, different in scale as they might be. Finally, I had not forgotten reading how in 1854, when the House of Lords' Committee of Privileges was hearing the claim of Sir Henry Paston Bedingfield to be co-heir to the abeyant barony of Grandison, counsel for the petitioner, in order to substantiate the Grandison pedigree, gave evidence (and I quote) 'of certain Charters which had been made to and by members of the Grandison family, and which had been preserved among the Muniments of the Counts of Savoy at Turin, the Lordship of Grandison having been formerly held under the Counts of Savoy; and . . . put in duly attested copies of those Documents'; numbering five in all, and dating from 1257 to 1303, they were sworn to by a barrister from Genoa who appeared before the Committee to testify in person that such deeds would be admitted in evidence in a nineteenth-century Sardinian court.[5] The Savoy archives at Turin certainly seemed to demand urgent investigation. Indeed, had not Galbreath's *Inventaire des sceaux vaudois* shown that one of the items they preserved was an instrument dated in 1279 at Evian, across the lake from Chillon, and still bearing the seal of John de

[1] C. L. Kingsford, 'Sir Otho de Grandison', *Trans. Royal Hist. Soc.* 3rd ser. iii (1909), 133.

[2] Description in Victor H. Bourgeois, *Les Châteaux historiques du canton de Vaud* (Bâle, 1935), 8–15.

[3] For Otto's tomb, see Marcel Grandjean, *Les Monuments d'art et d'histoire du canton de Vaud*, ii (Bâle, 1966); *La Cathédrale de Lausanne* (Berne, 1975), 50–1.

[4] To Sybil de Baugé (Ilio Jori, *Genealogia Sabauda* (Bologna, 1942), 34).

[5] Grandison Claim of Peerage, *Evidence and Documents, 1854–1858* (London, 1858), 166–74, cited in Kingsford, op. cit., p. 178, n. 2.

Bonvillars?[1] I could see no reason to doubt that this was the same John de Bonvillars as was already known to me as being engaged only four years later, in 1283, in supervising Edward's new castle works (*ad supervidendum castra*) in Wales, and to have been given the constableship of Harlech, then still being built, in 1285.[2]

Fig. 1. Seal of Sir John de Bonvillars, deputy justiciar of North Wales and constable of Harlech Castle 1285–7, enlarged from the original attached to a deed dated at Evian, 22 March 1279 (Turin, Archivio di Stato, Baronnie de Vaud 27, Mézières 1).

Accordingly it was to Turin that I went first, and I found the Bonvillars deed[3] and copied it. At that time I knew nothing, and alas in two days' work discovered nothing, of the existence of several Savoy household rolls, not unlike our contemporary English wardrobe and household accounts, nor of the survival of many thirteenth-century castellans' accounts, similar to our own Ministers' Accounts, for castellanies in many parts of Savoy. Thus it was with a feeling of having rather drawn a blank on the archives that I soon set off again to cross the Alps from Italy into

[1] Donald L. Galbreath, *Inventaire des sceaux vaudois*, Mémoires et Documents publiés par la Société de l'histoire de la Suisse romande (Lausanne, 1937), 49.

[2] For Sir John de Bonvillars, see *Eng. Hist. Rev.* xci. 79–97.

[3] Turin, Archivio di Stato (henceforth cited as AST), Baronnie de Vaud 27, Mezières 1; printed in *Eng. Hist. Rev.* xci. 95–6.

Switzerland to see if I might fare better with the castles. Within the next few days (20–4th September 1950) I visited for the first time the castles of Grandson and Chillon, Yverdon and Champvent, and stayed a night in the house that incorporates what is left of the Carthusian priory of La Lance, which Otto and Peter de Grandison founded in 1318–20 and where Otto's heart is reputedly buried. The 'breakthrough' came on 22 September, when a day spent in the University Library at Lausanne introduced me to Albert Naef's great study, *Chillon, La Camera Domini* (1908),[1] and Victor van Bercham's pioneer paper *La 'ville-neuve' d'Yverdon, Fondation de Pierre de Savoie* (1913),[2] both of them well-documented works by good scholars. 'This day's work has made it clear to me', I wrote in my diary, 'that I must go back to Turin, tedious journey as it will be, and look at the "comptes savoyardes" for myself and see how much early stuff there really is there.' My first week was gone and I had only one week left.

The following morning was spent at the castle of Yverdon (Plate XXXV*a*), one-time home of the first school of Pestalozzi, and today occupied as part school, part museum, and with extensive wine storage in the cellars below. Points of particular interest were the overall plan which, with its four-square ward, three corner towers attached and the fourth much larger and originally offset and detached, seemed to anticipate Flint (Plate XXXV*b* and *c*); indications that there had been tall angle garderobe shafts which seemed to anticipate one of the types we noted at Harlech (Plate XXX*a*); and remains of original segmental-headed and mullioned windows which in a simplified form might have anticipated Harlech also. I spent the afternoon at Champvent (Plate XXXVI*a*),[3] whose interest for us derives initially from the fact that it was the castle of Peter de Champvent, cousin of Otto de Grandison and another lifelong friend and servant of Edward I in England, Wales, Gascony, Scotland, and Flanders, a witness to the foundation borough charters of Flint, Conway, Caernarvon, and Beaumaris, and king's chamberlain from 1284 or earlier to 1298 or later.[4] The basic ground

[1] Albert Naef, *Chillon. Tome I, La Camera Domini: La Chambre des comtes et des ducs de Savoie à Chillon*, Genève, 1908.

[2] Victor van Berchem, 'La "ville-neuve" d'Yverdon, Fondation de Pierre de Savoie', in *Festgabe für Gerold Meyer von Knonau* (Zürich, 1913), 205–26.

[3] For Champvent, see Arthur Piaget, 'Le Château de Champvent et le comte Louis de Neuchâtel', *Musée Neuchâtelois*, 1937, 217–33.

[4] For Peter de Champvent, see Kingsford, op. cit., p. 180; T. F. Tout,

plan of Champvent is again that of Yverdon or Flint; the accommodation on the principal floor appears to have been almost exactly that of Edward and Eleanor's apartments at Conway—a south range joining at right angles with an east range which terminates in a chapel occupying the north-east corner tower.[1] As we shall see later, exactly the same arrangement, even to the orientation, appears to have obtained at Count Philip's palace-castle of St. Georges-d'Espéranche.[2] Champvent is, and probably always has been, an inhabited house; it is rendered with plaster, so that it still wears the same outward aspect of whiteness as did its North Wales analogues and of which Conway in particular still shows substantial traces (Plate XXXVI*b*). Having been the castle of a feudatory, however, it lacks, as does Grandson, the early documentation that illumines so many of the castles of the counts.

The next day, Sunday the 24th, was Chillon day. It is easier to remember, than to communicate, one's impressions on visiting this marvellous building for the first time, impressions no doubt coloured by those superimposed in a score of later visits, each adding some new piece to previous knowledge.[3] Here, surely beyond doubt, were the ancestors I was seeking of the Harlech fenestration, dating as I learned later from the middle 1260s (Plate XXXIII). In these matters one does not look for replicas and duplicates, but for parallels in essentials, and at Chillon and Harlech we surely have them. We have already noted how, where the dressings of the Harlech windows have perished, sufficient evidence has none the less survived to allow a faithful reconstruction; the Chillon dressings have, in fact, already been largely renewed by Naef, whose records show that he did the work with great sympathy and scrupulous accuracy.[4]

Chapters in Medieval Administrative History, vi (Manchester, 1933), 45, where the reference to him as chamberlain from 1292 can be advanced to 25 Sept. 1284, on which date he is named as 'camerarius noster' in the Liberate Roll of 12 Edward I (PRO, C62/60).

[1] Plan in Sidney Toy, 'The Town and Castle of Conway', *Archaeologia*, lxxxvi (1937), 189. The archetype of this whole Anglo-Savoyard group may have been the castle of Grandson, where the fourth tower of the thirteenth-century quadrangle was the pre-existing twelfth-century square donjon, now demolished.

[2] See below, pp. 279–80.

[3] The best short account of the castle is that by J.-P. Chapuisat: *Chillon, son histoire illustrée de documents iconographiques* (Lausanne, 1965).

[4] See his measured drawings of the original stonework in *La Camera Domini*, 20, 36, 37.

In English terms we might almost call the Chillon windows 'Harlech-type' windows, even though they are the earlier by twenty years; they occur throughout the Peter of Savoy work in the castle, and it was especially rewarding to row out in a little boat and discover them ranged on the side towards the lake, basking like their Merioneth counterparts in the strong light of the western sun (Plates XXXII*a* and XXXIII*a*). Later scrutiny at both castles was to show that the word 'counterpart' is used advisedly; for there is an inner similarity to match the outer, and it can also be shown to be as real as it is apparent. The diagram and table given below (fig 2) illustrate measurements taken

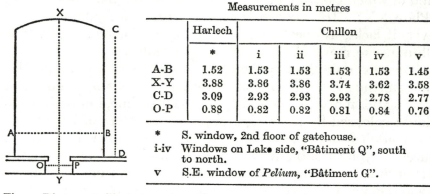

	Harlech	Chillon				
	*	i	ii	iii	iv	v
A-B	1.52	1.53	1.53	1.53	1.53	1.45
X-Y	3.88	3.86	3.86	3.74	3.62	3.58
C-D	3.09	2.93	2.93	2.93	2.78	2.77
O-P	0.88	0.82	0.82	0.81	0.84	0.76

Measurements in metres

*   S. window, 2nd floor of gatehouse.
i-iv Windows on Lake side, "Bâtiment Q", south to north.
v   S.E. window of *Pelium*, "Bâtiment G".

Fig. 2. Diagram to illustrate comparative measurements of windows at Harlech and Chillon.

independently by my friend M. Jean-Pierre Chapuisat in Switzerland and by myself in Wales. The difference between the dimensions of the selected Harlech window and the average of the corresponding dimensions of five selected windows at Chillon proved to be of the order of only 6 mm for dimension A–B, 15 cm for X–Y, 22 cm for C–D, and 7 cm for O–P. In each case the Harlech measurement is very slightly the greater, a discrepancy perhaps partly to be accounted for by the continued existence of surface rendering in the roofed and habitable rooms at Chillon in contrast to the open and weathered condition of ruined Harlech (Plate XXXIII*c* and *d*). It is hard to avoid the conclusion that these two sets of windows, although they are 950 miles apart, derive at least their dimensions, their frame design, and their relieving arches from a common pattern book, or a sketchbook such as Wilars de Honecourt's. It was only much later that I discerned the evidence, not easily seen, of helicoidal scaffolding having been used in building the flanking towers added by Peter of Savoy along Chillon's landward front.

It sounds like a forgotten era to recall that at 3.37 a.m. the next morning I was leaving Lausanne on the Orient Express for Arona, bound once more for Turin. The next $3\frac{1}{2}$ days, Tuesday to Friday the 26–9 September, were as productive of crucial sources as any I have ever spent. Suffice to say that through the great helpfulness of Signorina Dott. Augusta Lange, to whom my indebtedness at Turin both then and through the succeeding years merits more than mere footnote acknowledgement, I procured the three volumes of Chiaudano's *La Finanza Sabauda nel secolo XIII* (1935–8), which print *inter alia* the earliest surviving castellans' accounts for Chillon, Yverdon, and Saillon as well as a selection of Count Philip's household rolls.[1] This left me free to devote the little time I had left (the Archivio closed at 2 p.m.) to unprinted material covering roughly the decade 1268–78, especially the fragile and invaluable household rolls for the years 1273–9.

These few days produced six discoveries:

First, that the building of Yverdon, castle and new town together, was begun in May 1261 under a Master John the Mason and his son Master James; Master John was paid 12s. 0d. a week, i.e. at the same level as a Master Peter Mainier, the *custos operum domini* or 'keeper' of the count's works, while Master James received 10s. 6d.[2] By 1266–7 Master John had disappeared from the scene, a payment of £15 for $1\frac{1}{2}$ years' wages being then made to Master James alone.[3]

Second, that included in works payments recorded at Chillon in 1266–7 there is an unspecified item of £15 paid to a recipient whose name, 'Jacqueto de sancto Jorio', sounds uncommonly like 'James of St. George'.[4]

Third, that during the years 1271–5 the count's household

---

[1] The principal contents of the Turin archives are listed in Max Bruchet, 'Répertoire des sources de l'histoire de Savoie', extrait de la *Revue des Bibliothèques* (tirage à part, Paris, 1935, pp. 1–142).

[2] Mario Chiaudano, *La finanza sabauda nel sec. XIII* (3 vols., Torino, 1933–8, being vols. cxxxi–cxxxiii of Biblioteca della Società Storica Subalpina), i, 63 (henceforth cited as Chiaudano, *FS*); the passage is quoted in full in *Eng. Hist. Rev.* lxv. 453.

[3] AST, Inv. Sav. 70, fo. 205, mazzo 1, no. 1, 'In acquietancia Magistri Jacobi Cementarii hoc anno et de anno preterito, qui Jacobus percipit Yverdun' de domino in feud' decem lib. vien. singulis annis, xv. li.'

[4] AST, Inv. Sav. 69, fo. 5, mazzo 1, no. 4, *Idem liberavit Jaquetto de sancto Jorio per litteras domini xv. li.* If, as seems likely, this and the entry quoted in the preceding note refer to an identical payment, then we have here the only reference so far discovered in Savoy records to Master James the mason as being 'of St. George'.

rolls show many payments of expenses to *Magister Jacobus lathomus* in respect of travel all over Savoy, often to places where works are evidently in progress.

Fourth, that one such place, namely St. Georges-d'Espéranche, in the Viennois, south-east of Lyon, is coming to the fore in the early 1270s with the building there of a new 'palace castle' by Count Philip, giving rise to the possibility that it might be from *this* St. Georges that the Master James who makes his début in English records in 1278 took or was given his local surname.[1]

Fifth, the Christian name 'Ambrosia', which English records show was the name of the North Wales Master James's wife, is sometimes encountered in Savoy records.[2]

Sixth, that the earliest castellan's account for Saillon shows that the building of the new tower there (Plate XXV*e*) in 1261 was entrusted as a task (*ad taschiam*) to a certain Francis the mason (not a master, simply *Franciscus Cementarius*) by a Sir John Masot, who later, in the 1270s, appears frequently as a travelling companion of Master James and is sometimes associated with him (as, for example, at St. Laurent-du-Pont in 1274) in the assignment of works 'tasks' and the awarding of contracts;[3] Sir John's function at Saillon is to settle the form of the tower (*ad turrim de Sallon devisandam*) and see to its positioning (*ad supervidendum situm turris*)[4] and, presumably, to draw up appropriate agreements with Franciscus. Saillon was the very castle whose affinity to Conway had by now more than once struck me from the railway. I reflected that, besides this evidence, printed by Chiaudano, for its tower having been built by this mason named Francis, an unprinted Chillon account of 1266 listing payments to masons, carpenters, and others included one of 75*s.* to a John Francis (*Johanni Francisco*);[5] and I recalled also that in our own Conway accounts of 1286 a John Francis (*Johanni Franceys*), also not styled 'master', twice appears as the first name

---

[1] *Ant. Journ.* xxxiii. 33–40. In a letter of 3 Feb. 1952 apropos James of St. George the late Louis Blondel writes, 'Comme j'ai pu le remarquer très souvent les maîtres d'œuvres sont désignés d'après le *dernier* grand chantier où ils ont travaillé. Or il n'est pas douteux que le château de St. Georges construit entre 1270–1272 était le plus important à ce moment-là.'

[2] e.g. 'Ambrosia, uxor Petri Bonivardi', burgess of Chambéry (Archs. Depts. de la Savoie, Chambéry, Inv. 65, fo. 1).

[3] Archives de la Savoie, Chambéry, Inv. 32, fo. 14, no. 66; just as we find Sir John de Bonvillars and Master James of St. George associated in assigning tasks ten years later at Conway (*Eng. Hist. Rev.* xci. 86).

[4] Chiaudano, *FS,* i. 58, 59, 68.

[5] AST, Inv. Sav. 69, fo. 5, mazzo 1, no. 3(c).

in lists of contractors undertaking particular 'tasks' on Conway town walls under Master James of St. George.[1] We last hear of this 'Conway' John Francis at Beaumaris under Master James in 1296;[2] if he were then, say, 70, he would have been 60 at Conway in 1286, 40 at Chillon in 1266, 35 at Saillon in 1261, and 31 at Conthey and Brignon (where he was probably the builder of Peter of Savoy's now vanished *turres*) in 1257.[3] Was it, is it, too much to think that perhaps we are dealing with one and the same life all through?

It was thus towards Saillon that I headed when I left Turin and crossed the Alps northwards again on 28 September, briefly visiting *en route* the site of Conthey and the castle and the Valère, the former cathedral of the bishops of Sion, famous for its fourteenth-century organ. It was the bishops of Sion who in the mid thirteenth century were the principal opponents in the Valais of the expansionist counts, and the towers of Conthey and Brignon, Saillon and La Bâtiaz built by Count Peter in the years preceding his succession in 1263, and the tower of Saxon built by Count Philip in 1279–80, bear witness to a long-drawn conflict.[4] Saillon, La Bâtiaz, and Saxon all proved to have much to contribute to the final story.

Saillon, like Chillon, at once revealed examples of the architectural parallels I was seeking. The simple round-headed gate arches of the town walls, for which the castellan's accounts give a firm date of 1257–8 (Plate XXVIII*a* and *b*), bear striking resemblance to the form of the entrance arch through the outer curtain at Harlech, as also to the great internal arch in the southern tower of the Harlech gatehouse (Plates XXVII*b* and XXVIII*c* and *d*). The donjon, securely dated to 1261, is of helicoidal construction, has a round-headed entrance door, and, like the towers of Conway castle, rises compass-perfect despite the irregularity of the rocky crag on which it sits (Plate XXV*e*). As with the towers of the North Wales castles generally, it was floored on close-set joists integrated into the original building and not stone vaulted at any level. Though the curtain and its

[1] PRO, E101/485/28; one of the passages referred to is reproduced in facsimile in *Archaeologia Cambrensis* cxix (1970), Plate II (a).

[2] PRO, E372/158, rot. 48.

[3] Chiaudano, *FS*, i, 26, where payment is recorded to him of £20 for a new building beside the keep at Conthey, '. . . pro tascheria nove camere iuxta turrim de Conteis . . .'.

[4] For the political background, see Victor van Berchem, 'Les dernières campagnes de Pierre II, comte de Savoie, en Valais et en Suisse', *Revue hist. vaudoise*, 1907, tome XV.

278 PROCEEDINGS OF THE BRITISH ACADEMY

flanking towers are slighter and on a smaller scale than Conway's in the proportion of voids to solids and in details like the vaulting of embrasure heads there is a remarkable sameness between them (Plate XXXVIII*a* and *b*). Granted the difference in scale and terrain, the siting and conception of the Conway walls could well reflect the application of the same principles as those followed at Saillon twenty-five years earlier (Plate XXXVII). Even today, with its narrow alleys and passages within and its big rough-timbered barns and storehouses without its weathered and partly hidden walls, Saillon has extraordinary charm and tranquillity, and in its tiny way seems still to retain a feeling of continuity uninterrupted from medieval times.[1]

La Bâtiaz, the castle of Martigny, crowns a similar spur of rock about 7 miles down the Rhône from Saillon, not far from where the main river is joined by the Durance; its position high above the great Rhône bend affords extensive views northwards towards St. Maurice, eastwards towards Sion, and southwards up the entrance to the valley of the Great St. Bernard, the ancient road to which crosses the Durance immediately below the castle rock. The castle of La Bâtiaz was surrendered to Peter of Savoy by the Bishop of Sion after a siege in 1260, and there is documentary evidence which suggests the keep may have been building in 1265; in any event it is a product of the same *chantier* as Saillon, and here the evidence of helicoidal construction is even more plain to see. La Bâtiaz was afterwards recovered by the bishops, who undertook extensive repairs to its other buildings in 1280–1; we shall have occasion to look at these later.[2]

In September 1951, almost exactly a year after that first trial run, the help of a Leverhulme travel grant enabled me to return and devote a whole month to exploring other parts of Savoy and other archives. Indeed, the frequent mentions of St. Georges-d'Espéranche in the household rolls of the 1270s, and the fact that works which had once had their own building accounts had been in progress there in 1270–2,[3] were already turning my mind in that direction even before I left Turin for the second time in 1950. When I reached home the potential significance of St. Georges at once became apparent to me from Sir Maurice

[1] For a short account, with plan and illustrations, see André Donnet, *Saillon, bourg médiéval* (*Trésors de mon Pays*, Neuchâtel, 1950).

[2] For the castle of La Bâtiaz, see A. Donnet et Louis Blondel, *Châteaux de Valais* (Olten, 1963), 121–4.

[3] *Eng. Hist. Rev.* lxv. 457, n. 2.

Powicke's references to it in *Henry III and the lord Edward*, a book then only six years old.[1] For it was actually at this St. Georges, on Sunday, 25 June 1273, that the 66-year-old Count Philip did homage to his great-nephew Edward, the 34-year-old uncrowned king of England, for the nominal overlordship of those Alpine towns and castles enumerated earlier, through two of which, Avigliana and Susa, Edward and his knights would have ridden not many days before on their homeward journey from the Crusade.[2] A little before Susa the old road passed close beside the church and castle of S. Giorio in Val di Susa. This is relevant to our subject, as the castle provides a parallel for battlementing decked with triple finials, as at Conway (Plate XXXI); it is also remarkable for the extent ot which the medieval rendering has survived on the surface of its rubble walls, as well as for a gate arch bright with coloured voussoirs, and with traces of surmounting coloured shields of arms.[3]

When I eventually arrived in St. Georges-d'Espéranche myself the first thing to catch my eye was an obelisk flanked by two Union Jacks, erected by the French Resistance to the memory of seven English airmen who had fallen to their deaths over St. Georges in 1943. As I soon learned, it had been placed, doubtless quite unknowingly, almost on the site of the castle entrance through which Edward I must have passed seven centuries ago, a poignant reminder of Trevelyan's poetry of history.[4] Let me explain, as shortly as I may, in the light of this and eight further visits in subsequent years, what St. Georges once was and what it is now. A sketch-plan of 1794 preserved in the Archives de l'Isère at Grenoble shows that the castle was quadrangular with attached octagonal towers at the corners; the main buildings were ranged along the south and

[1] Above, p. 269, n. 3.

[2] There are several references in the castellans' accounts to King Edward's progress, as, for example, in that of Albert de Bagnol, bailiff of Savoy and keeper of the castle of Montmélian, for the year beginning Thursday, 12 January 1273: *In expensis domini Alberti ballivi euntis obviam domino Regi Anglie in Maurienna, xx. sol. Navigantibus qui transierunt dominum Regem per Yseram, ultra illud quod solutum eis fuerat per dominum Bosonem, de mandato domini comitis, v. sol.* (Archs. Depts. de la Savoie, Inv. 51, fo. 257, mazzo 1).

[3] For history and description, see Eugenio Olivero, *Il Castello e la Casa Forte di S. Giorio in Val di Susa* (Torino, 1925), for a copy of which I have to thank the late Dott. Ing. Guglielmo Lange of Turin. A single centre finial of this type remains on one of the towers added to the precinct wall of St. Mary's Abbey, York after 1318 (RCHM, *City of York*, vol. 2 (1972), 160–1, and Plate 58).

[4] G. M. Trevelyan, *An Autobiography and other Essays* (London, 1949), 13.

east sides and faced on to a square courtyard, the north wall of which contained the entrance gateway. Thus the residential blocks were planned, and orientated, exactly as at Champvent and Conway, leading one to wonder whether here too the north-east tower may have contained a chapel (Plate XXXIX). The plan was concentric, in that the built quadrangle was surrounded by a sloping berm, perhaps 30–40 feet in width, with this in turn enclosed by a water-filled moat said to have been 30–50 feet wide and 10–18 feet deep, but there does not appear to have been an outer curtain between berm and ditch. This, and the fact that all the walls, those of the towers included, were only 5–6 feet thick, emphasizes that St. Georges was much more a *palacium* (as the records sometimes name it), much more a *château de plaisance* than a true *château fort*. Two of the towers remained standing to full height until about the middle of the nineteenth century, but today only the south-east tower is left, standing to two-thirds of its original height, together with a fragment of the south and most of the adjacent east range, both much altered. Indeed, the east range has long been divided up into a warren of separate dwellings, mutilating but not wholly obliterating the medieval structure; their gardens usefully keep open the site of the berm or outer ward on this side. In particular there remain valuable traces of original door-heads and fenestration, the former including a characteristic semicircular arch, the latter proving to be almost identical with that of Yverdon. It is also not impossible that a window recess in the south-east tower may preserve the form and dimension of the thirteenth-century embrasure that preceded it; if so, comparison with Harlech is apposite (Plate XXIXa and b). Most significant of all is the garderobe shaft that occupies the tower's adjacent eastern re-entrant angle, and whose measurements proved on comparison to correspond to within a few centimetres with those of the similar adjunct to the north-west tower at Harlech (Plate XXXa and b).[1]

When I was first at St. Georges in 1951 I was told[2] of the survival in the Archives de la Savoie at Chambéry of a contract made at St. Georges in the year 1278 for masonry work at the neighbouring castle of Falavier (Plate XLIIa). Falavier's stand-

---

[1] 'The Castle of St. Georges-d'Espéranche', *Ant. Journ.* xxxiii. 33–47; Plate XI (c) reproduces the original 1794 plan on which our own plan (Plate XXXIXa) is based.

[2] By the late Dr. Joseph Saunier of Heyrieux, physician and antiquary, who gave me the greatest possible help and kindness at St. Georges.

ing remains are heavily overgrown and it was not possible to recognize the works in question, if indeed they still remain. The contract is none the less of much interest in itself, for its date, for the form of the agreement with Boso the count's chaplain, for the name and style of the contractor 'Taxinus de sancto Georgio lathomus', and the survival of fragments of Boso's and Tassin's seals, the latter bearing a mason's toothed hammer-axe and remains of the legend 'S. TASS . . .'.[1] Little or nothing now remains of the other three castles in the Viennois, La Côte St. André (*Costa*), Voiron, and St. Laurent du Pont (Sanctus Laurentius in Deserto), where works are mentioned in the household rolls of the early 1270s.

Let us now return to the Valais, as I myself did in 1951, and look again at La Bâtiaz, this time not at Peter of Savoy's *donjon circulaire* but at a detail of the buildings adjacent to it built or rebuilt by Bishop Pierre d'Oron of Sion in 1281. We have no accounts for this work, but in March 1281 the Sion chapter agreed to grant the bishop the first-fruits of vacant benefices, '*cum episcopus sumptuosum opus inceperit in castro Martigniaci*'.[2] Earlier we remarked that at Harlech there are two specially distinctive garderobe types and we have just noted one of them paralleled at St. Georges. Here at La Bâtiaz we find a parallel to the other in the shape of a corresponding pair of projecting constructions which probably belong to this work of 1281. Though less well preserved and built of a different stone, the shoots at La Bâtiaz are essentially of similar pattern and similar corbelled form, and are similarly positioned, to the shoot at Harlech. The Harlech and La Bâtiaz shoots are the only known examples of their kind (Plate XXX*c* and *d*).

Five miles from La Bâtiaz stands the rock of Saxon,[3] which I visited for the first of many times, in a quick dash up the hill and down again, between trains, on 27 September 1951. It is only

[1] Archs. Depts. de la Savoie, Chambéry, Inv. 135, fo. 17, pacquet 14, pièce 7. 'Ce nom de *Tassin* est du nord d'Italie ou de la Lombardie en partie dans les états de Savoie ... Tasse est avec St. Victor un des saints de Milan' (Louis Blondel, 3 Feb. 1952). The name 'Ambrosia' is also derived from the Milanese St. Ambrose.

[2] Abbé J. Gremaud, *Méms. de la Soc. d'histoire de la Suisse romande*, tome XXX, 298–9.

[3] The authoritative account of Saxon is by Louis Blondel, 'Le château de Saxon', *Vallesia*, ix (Sion, 1954), 165–74 and X. 87–8. It was the late M. Blondel, at that time the doyen of antiquarian studies in western Switzerland, who first drew my attention to Saxon, as well as giving much other help and advice. Amongst many papers on the castles of the region, his

gradually that I have since come to realize that a relationship between the building and the builders of this tower in 1279–80, and the buildings begun in North Wales in 1282–3, is perhaps more convincingly demonstrable, both visually and in terms of records, than is the case with any of the other instances we have considered up till now. For the tower of Saxon, the *turris Sayssonis*, we not only still have the tower itself in a good state of preservation, but we also have in the Archivio at Turin two detailed and well-preserved castellan's accounts relating to its construction.[1] Next day, therefore, I crossed the Great St. Bernard by bus, a journey unforgettable for the drove upon drove of bedecked and tinkling cattle winding their slow way down to the valley for the winter, spent a day looking at the castles of Aosta and Châtel Argent, both with round towers built by the helicoidal method,[2] and then went on to spend five days in the Via S. Chiara at Turin, copying amongst others the two Saxon accounts in question.

It is Saxon and its documentation that must now claim our attention. First the structure. Being dated precisely by the accounts to the years 1279–80, it comes closer in time than do any others we have considered hitherto to the castles begun in North Wales in the ensuing decade, and the resemblances are close; for example, the round-arched doorway (Plate XXV*b*), the perfectly graded batter (Plate XXV*a*), support for the floor joists provided at each level by two parallel cross beams,[3] and a classic exemplification of helicoidal construction, with some of the putlogs still sound and in place (Plate XXV*a* and *b*). It is fortunate indeed that we should still have contemporary records of such a building's erection in considerable detail. Here we can only note what they have to tell us of some of the principal contractors, in whose identity perhaps lies the most conclusive endorsement of the relationship between the building of these additions to the little Savoy castles and the building of the much bigger and more elaborate North Wales castles which it was the purpose of my exploration to attempt to establish. We need

'L'Architecture militaire au temps de Pierre II de Savoie, Les Donjons circulaires' (*Genava*, xiii (1935), 271–321) is of first importance, surpassed only in scale by his great study of the *Châteaux de l'ancien diocèse de Genève* (Genève, 1956).

    [1] AST, Inv. 69, fo. 69, mazzo 1, no. 1; ibid., fo. 5, mazzo 1, no. 7.
    [2] AST, Inv. 68, fo. 2, mazzo 1, no. 2 is a detailed works account for Châtel Argent.
    [3] For plans and sections see L. Blondel, 'Château de Saxon', *Vallesia*, ix. 173.

concern ourselves with three names only, viz. first Tassin of St. George whom we have already come across at Falavier; second, Giles or Gilet, whose full style is given as '*Giletus de sancto Georgio lathomus*' and who is Tassin's brother; and third, someone whose name is given as '*Beynardus rex ribaldorum*', who shares with another a payment of £18. 5*s*. for digging the tower's foundation, and whose picturesque title means, in a building context, the man in charge of the barrows and hand-carts, 'celui qui dirige les brouettes'.[1]

These last two names Giletus and Beynardus, provide, I believe, a link which takes us back to Wales, where our journey began, bringing us first to Llanbadarn, i.e. Aberystwyth. By the merest accident, indeed thanks solely to a clerical blunder which though erased was fortunately not obliterated, our own records have preserved a reference,[2] given in facsimile below (Plate XLII*b*), to the presence at Aberystwyth castle in September 1282 of an individual who it is hard to believe is not identical with 'Giletus de sancto Georgio lathomus'. If 'Egidius' is synony-mous with 'Giletus', and 'cementarius' for all practical purposes with 'lathomus'—and who will deny that they are?—then here at Aberystwyth, not so very long after we left him at Saxon, we are surely with our friend Giles of St. George again, and he is now 'Master' or 'Mr.' Giles. And what has been happening in the meantime? What has happened is this. Last Palm Sunday, 22 March 1282, the Welsh princes Llywelyn and Dafydd launched a well-concerted revolt, laid siege to the castles of Flint and Rhuddlan, and a day or two later sacked the unfinished castle of Aberystwyth.[3] Count Philip's nephew Amadeus of Savoy, captain of King Edward's army at Chester, raised the siege of Rhuddlan but then had to return to his own country on account of the death of his brother Thomas.[4] Not only are unfinished or damaged castles standing in need of completion or repair, but bigger and stronger castles are going to have to be built, castles that will bring Snowdonia into the king's peace once and for all, and additional professional help is going to be needed in the

[1] Ibid., x. 87; cf. *Hist. King's Wks.* ii. 1038–9.

[2] PRO, C47/2/4, m. 3. Entry of payment in September 1282, '*Magistro Egidio de Sancto Georgio Cementario pro vadiis suis . . . per xx. dies . . . xx.s.*' cancel-led, because entered more appropriately on his own expenses roll, now lost.

[3] For the political background, see J. Goronwy Edwards (ed.), *Littere Wallie* (Cardiff, 1940), lxi–lxix.

[4] 'A letter from Lewis of Savoy to Edward I', *Eng. Hist. Rev.* lxviii. 55–62.

planning and the building of them. There is much to suggest
that in the emergency of 1282 Edward did indeed invoke the
help of Count Philip, at once his 'man' in feudal, his great-uncle
in family terms. In a letter dated 26 August 1282 his mother,
Queen Eleanor of Provence, reminded Edward how in some
unspecified time of crisis Philip had come to his aid, and how
friendly he had been to him in 1273 when the king was returning
from Crusade: 'Et pensez comme il vous fut ami en votre grant
besoigne d'Angleterre et au moment ou vous veniez d'Outre-
mer.'[1] That the master of the works, Master James, should go
to Aberystwyth in May, as he did, to see to the resumption of
the building of the castle[2] is natural enough; but it can only be
against something like the background outlined above that we
can explain the arrival of Master Giles from Savoy in June. The
two men must already have been at least known to one another.
How well known can only be a matter of speculation, and it is
one upon which we shall touch again before we conclude.

Meanwhile, what of 'Beynardus rex', the 'officer i/c carts and
carters' (if we may so describe him) at Saxon? One can only
repeat a suggestion already made elsewhere, namely that he is to
be identified with a so-named 'rex dictus Adam' who receives a
Christmas box of £5 from Count Amadeus in 1296, and that he
turns up under a combination of the two names as 'Adam
Boynard' at Harlech in the 1286 particulars account, having
probably come with Giles of St. George to Aberystwyth in
1282.[3] That there was an ex-Aberystwyth element in the
Harlech work force is indicated by the presence of a William de
Lanpader, and when we encounter the names Adam Boynard
and Gilet together at Harlech in 1286, in lists of contractors
whose horses have been employed in carting building materials
to the site (Plate XLIIc),[4] it is hard not to suppose that 'Gilet'
may be none other than the 'Giletus de sancto Georgio' of the
Saxon accounts alias the 'Magister Egidius de sancto Georgio'
of the Aberystwyth account. Harlech's full-centred arches, its
many indications of inclined scaffolds, its 'Chillon' windows,

---

[1] Quoted in Francois Mugnier, 'Les Savoyards en Angleterre au XIIIᵉ
siècle', *Mémoires de la Société Savoisienne*, tome XXIX (Chambéry, 1890),
333–4.

[2] *Hist. King's Works*, i. 304.

[3] *Genava*, N.S. xi. 307–8. At the same time as the payment of 100s. 'Regi
dicto Adam', another of 50s. was made to a William of Pontefract the coach-
man ('quadrigario'), and Richard his companion 'redeuntibus in Angliam'
(AST, Inv. 38, fo. 46, mazzo 2, no. 5).

[4] PRO, E101/485/26, printed in full in *Hist. King's Wks.*, ii. 1030–5.

its St. Georges- and Bâtiaz-type garderobe shoots, its little rectangular staircase lights which are replicas of those at Saxon— all these seem to postulate a strong Savoy element in the castle's conception and execution, and may be indicative of the presence of others from that background besides the controlling figures of Master James of St. George and Sir John de Bonvillars, of whose close association at Harlech I have written in another place.[1]

I think that by now I have explained the stages by which my exploration of buildings and documents came to convince me of the reality of the connection between North Wales and Savoy. I should now like to examine the question of possible family relationships between some of the principal personalities. Early in our inquiry, at Yverdon in 1261, we found two masters, John and James, working side by side and named as father and son. Twenty-one years later, at Aberystwyth in 1282, we have again found ourselves in the presence of two masters, James and Giles, having 'St. George' as their common surname. During the interval, in what are at best but intermittent and imperfectly examined records, we only once (in 1266 at Chillon) found this local surname applied to a Savoy James, but in our English records, from 1278 onwards, it is applied to the North Wales James increasingly and eventually almost always. Assuming that it is with only one James that we are dealing, what is likely to have been his age when he first appears, already a 'master', in the company of a father probably by then well on in years, in 1261? Allowing for an apprenticeship of seven years from age 15, he would not have been less than 22, which would make the year of his birth 1239, the same as that of Edward I, and his age at death in 1309[2] 70. Yet the Savoyards tended towards long life: Otto de Grandison was at least 90 at his death in 1328 and his brother William must have achieved much the same tally at his death in 1339.[3] Master James of St. George may easily have lived to be well over 70. Let us therefore assume instead that he was at least 80 in 1309 and 32 or more in 1261. If he married at the age of 25 this would then have been not later than 1254, so that a further step into the realm of controlled conjecture would give 1255 as a likely date for the birth of his eldest child. Supposing that child to have been Tassin, and Giles to have been two years younger, they would have been 25 and 23 respectively at Saxon in 1280, and Giles would have been 25 at

<hr>

[1] *Eng. Hist. Rev.* xc. 91–5.   [2] Ibid. lxv. 452.
[3] C. L. Kingsford, op. cit., 170, 174.

Aberystwyth in 1282, not too young an age to have been a 'master' if he served his apprenticeship from age 15 or thereabouts, particularly with so distinguished a father. Thus it is not impossible—at present we can put it no higher—that the Master James of St. George and the Master Giles of St. George who appear briefly together at Aberystwyth in the records of 1282 were father and son, like Master John and Master James at Yverdon in 1261; if so, Giles would in all likelihood have been apprenticed under his father during the busy castle-building period at St. Georges-d'Espéranche and elsewhere in the Viennois during the early 1270s. This allows us to suppose that the other son, Tassin, remained behind to represent the family and carry on the family profession in Savoy, where indeed we can in fact still trace him, as 'Tassinus lathomus', at Chillon in 1286–7 and Geneva in 1288,[1] and as 'Magister' Tassinus at Treffort in 1291–2.[2] As to the subsequent career of Master Giles, a possibility—it can be no more—is that he is the 'Master Giles the mason' named at Edinburgh in 1304 (with Walter of Hereford and others previously in North Wales) in the context of preparations for the coming siege of Stirling castle.[3]

We may thus here be in the presence not of two but of three generations of master masons, Master John (d. after 1261 and before 1268), Master James (d. 1309), and Master James's sons Master Tassin and Master Giles. What, then, can be said of the grandfather, Master John? A great deal can be said of *a* Master John, and it has lately been brilliantly said in the writings of M. Marcel Grandjean, the Professor of Regional Art History at the University of Lausanne. Professor Grandjean has shown, on the evidence of Lausanne chapter records, that the *magister operis Lausannensis* of the second quarter of the thirteenth century, the master responsible for the latest, more westerly parts of Lausanne Cathedral, was a Master John, to whom there are no fewer than nineteen references, mostly in the cathedral cartulary, between 1210 and 1318, the first five belonging to a time before 1225 when not *he*, but *his* father was *magister operis*, while the last four indicate that by 1268 he was no longer alive; the remainder, dating from 1227 to 1236, show Master John in office as 'master of the Lausanne work', which office he may well have continued to hold, in the absence of his having been superseded or of his being deceased before the mid 1260s, for some, perhaps

[1] AST, Inv. 69, fo. 5, mazzo 1, no. 9.
[2] Archives de la Côte d'Or, Dijon, B.7083.
[3] Bain, *Cal. Docts. relating to Scotand*, ii. p. 399.

many years longer. What is of particular interest is that in July 1234 the chapter assigned to Master John land and ground for a house in their own newly founded *ville-neuve* of St. Prex, on the lakeside eight miles to the west of Lausanne, on condition that he and his eldest son after him should continue to occupy it at an annual rent to the chapter of 10*s*. Only a few months afterwards, in 1236, we find John named both as *magister operacionis Lausannensis* and *castellanus sancti Prothasii*, i.e. in effect the chapter's resident commandant and administrator of their new-built defended town, of whose layout and defences he may well himself, as M. Grandjean suggests, have been the planner and constructor.[1]

When we turn from the Lausanne chapter's St. Prex of 1234 to Peter of Savoy's Yverdon of 1261,[2] we find the records provide us with a valuable statement of the terms of employment of three men who will be principally responsible for the new works.[3] Presumably the most important of the three is the one mentioned first, namely Master John the mason; we may note that the account does not by implication downgrade John by saying that he gets the same pay as Master Peter Mainier the *custos operum domini*, but rather the reverse—Peter Mainier is to

[1] Marcel Grandjean, 'A propos de la construction de la cathédrale de Lausanne (XII–XIIIᵉ siècle); notes sur la chronologie et les maîtres d'œuvre', *Genava*, N.S. tome XI (Genève, 1963), 261–87; *La Cathédrale de Lausanne* (Berne, 1975), 47–8. One of the posthumous references (1270) gives Master John's surname as 'Cotereel' ('. . . *tenementum quod fuit magistri Johannis dicti Cotereel* . . .'); according to M. Grandjean (p. 278) the name is foreign to the Pays de Vaud and its vicinity, but is found as a place-name in north-east and north-west France, in Flanders, Brabant, and as far away as England. Nevertheless we may note (i) that in 1271–2 the castellan of Rue, in the Pays de Vaud, accounts for a render of oats paid 'apud Cotterel' (Chiaudano, *FS*, i. 214), and (ii) the existence in Veytaux of a lane named 'Chemin de Cotterd' leading off the old road from Lausanne to Chillon. It is also not without interest to note the name Jacobus de Coterel' in one of the lists of recipients of livery gowns distributed by King Henry III to a variety of royal servants at Christmas 1261 (*Close Rolls, Henry III*, xi (1261–4), 15). For the probability that Master John's father was also 'magister operis Lausannensis' before him and the possibility that the father (who would thus have been Master James's grandfather) had served under William of Sens or William the Englishman at Canterbury, see Grandjean, *Genava*, N.S. xi. 275 and note; for the Canterbury/Lausanne relationship, see Jean Bony, 'The resistance to Chartres in early thirteenth-century architecture', *Journ. of Brit. Arch. Assn.*, 3rd ser., xx–xxi (1957–8), 35–52, esp. 47–8.

[2] For the early history, see Roger Déglon, *Yverdon au Moyen Âge* (Lausanne, 1949), 17–31.

[3] Chiaudano, *FS*, i. 63; cf. above, p. 8, and n. 27

get the same pay as Master John. And yet it is this Peter Mainier whom the Swiss archaeologists and art historians from Albert Naef onwards have again and again insisted, as I believe quite wrongly, on calling 'le véritable architecte et ingénieur militaire de Pierre II',[1] the chief architect and designer and builder of his castles. The 'keeper' or 'warden' of the works is not rightly to be confused with their 'master', who is the skilled professional practitioner. Peter Mainier's position in regard to the works of Yverdon, Chillon, and Romont, all three of which seem to be implicitly covered by the 1261 statement, is no different to that of, say, William de Perton or Nicholas Bonel in regard to the Flint and Rhuddlan works between 1277 and 1286, or of John of Candover at Conway in 1283–4.[2] Essentially they were all of them clerks of works and accounting and supply officers, not craftsmen or professionals. When we give to the position of Master John, which is implicit in the 1261 statement, the evaluation it evidently deserves, the possibility—to put it no higher—that he is the same John as the *magister operis Lausannensis* can hardly be excluded; clearly it would be no novelty for one with the experience of having planned and started St. Prex to be entrusted near the end of his life by Count Peter with the planning and founding of Yverdon. Moreover, while the ground-plans of the two towns are far from being duplicates,—they occupy very different sites and are twenty-five years apart in date—nevertheless they have certain basic characteristics in common; each has a layout based on three streets radiating from a point near the south-eastern extremity of the site; both are fully provided with water defences, St. Prex's (fig. 3) mainly natural and partly man-made, Yverdon's (fig. 4) mainly man-made and partly natural; the parallelism of their orientation is striking. And, if we are right in our thinking, there is a parallelism too between a versatile father who builds great churches, lays out new towns, and is put in command at St. Prex by the chapter of Lausanne, and a versatile son who builds great castles, lays out towns, and is put in command of Harlech or at Linlithgow by the king of England.[3] Occasionally, as in the resemblance of the end hall window of the castle of Conway to

[1] Albert Naef, op. cit., 33. Naef's work is well documented, but as an architect he would not have been equipped to distinguish between the roles of the 'custos' and the 'magister' of the count's works.

[2] A. J. Taylor, 'Castle-building in Wales . . . the prelude to construction', 105, 108 and notes.

[3] *Eng. Hist. Rev.* lxv. 451.

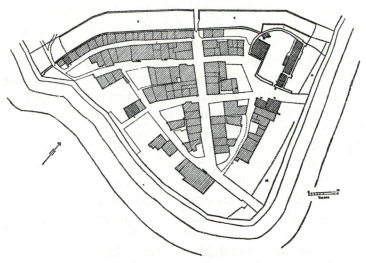

Fig. 3. Plan of town of St. Prex (Vaud) in about 1741 (from Marcel Grandjean, '... la construction de la Cathédrale de Lausanne ... la chronologie et les maîtres d'œuvre,' *Genava* n.s. xi (Genève, 1963), 283.

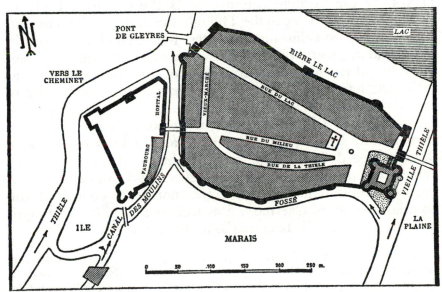

Fig. 4. Plan of town of Yverdon (Vaud) in about 1686 (from Roger Déglon, *Yverdon au Moyen Âge* (Lausanne, 1949), xxiii.

the western window of the cathedral of Lausanne, the military architect may reflect the source of his inspiration (Plate XLI*a* and *b*).[1]

Master James of St. George's versatility would scarcely be in

[1] One wonders whether Master Bernard de Sancto Georgio, master

question even were there only Flint and Rhuddlan, Conway, Harlech, and Beaumaris to make up the sum of his surviving achievement in Wales. It was Thomas Rickman who first remarked on the contrast between Caernarvon's polygonal towers and angular planning and the rounded towers of the others,[1] and the view has often been expressed that the explanation is to be sought in a different architectural authorship. I have stated elsewhere the grounds for believing that, on the contrary, the real explanation is the much more fundamental one of the king's intention that Caernarvon, as the capital of a new dynasty of English princes, should be a palace-castle, reflecting in its symbolism its own Roman origins and using the likeness of the Theodosian walls of Constantinople to invoke the imperial theme (Plate XL).[2] Moreover, all the documentation that we have points to the conclusion that Master James's over-all responsibility as *magister operacionum Wallie* was undivided, and, no matter how able and experienced may have been such colleagues as Richard of Chester or Walter of Hereford, Caernarvon as the prestige commission is the one least likely of all to have been delegated.[3] Though the style is different and the degree of embellishment greater, the resemblances both in detail and in general plan to Conway are unmistakable. It is not to be forgotten that versatility is one of the marks of the great architect: few looking for the first time at Barry's Houses of Parliament, the Reform Club House in Pall Mall, and the Quadrangle at Devonport dockyard would guess, or perhaps even readily believe, that they were all products of the same drawing-board. It would be a poor tribute to hold that Master James, given the great site differences and widely different commissioning requirements, could not have conceived the palatial majesty of Caernarvon as well as the military strength of Conway, Harlech, Beaumaris, and the rest.

mason at Bordeaux Cathedral in the 1360s (Archives de Gironde, sér. G, fo. 240v° and sér. H, no. 6, fo. 11v°), may perhaps have been a descendant. In 1314 Pope Clement V, Edward I's former clerk Bertrand del Goth, Archbishop of Bordeaux 1300-5?, left a bequest of 100 florins to a Bertrand de Sancto Georgio. A Perreninus de Sancto Georgio, *macon*, was working at the castle of Poligny (Jura) in 1429 (P. Brune, *Dict. des artistes et ouvriers d'art de la Franche-Comté*, Paris, 1912, p. 259).

[1] Thomas Rickman, *An Attempt to discriminate the styles of Architecture in England*, 3rd edn. (London, 1825), 362. The castle of Henry de Lacy earl of Lincoln at Denbigh also has polygonal towers but is without the coloured stone banding that distinguishes Caernarvon.

[2] *Hist. King's Wks.* i. 369-71.   [3] Ibid. 391-3.

In availing himself of specialists from abroad to carry through the great building programme in Wales Edward I was following accustomed practice. We have only to recall the origins of his doctors and surgeons, Simon and Philip of Beauvais; of his lawyers, the Accursii of Bologna; of his bankers, the Riccardi of Lucca or the Bardi and Frescobaldi of Florence; of his saddler, Felyseus of Paris;[1] of the German miners employed to search for copper near Dyserth in Flintshire;[2] of the canal expert Master Walter of Flanders, employed to make the moat at the Tower of London,[3] or of Master Manasser of Vaucouleurs to order the ditch-digging at Caernarvon;[4] and that even Edward's musician, Guilottus *vidulator*, sounds like an Italian, whilst the thousand Welsh minstrels who came to play to the king and queen at Overton, when Nevin was over, in 1284, doubtless also gave of their native best.[5] When it came to the castle-building it is true that the workmen, as Sir Goronwy reminded us,[6] were brought mainly from England, masons, carpenters, and diggers coming in their tens and fifties and hundreds from every corner of the land; but it need cause no surprise, that with Amadeus, and Otto, and Peter de Champvent to advise and recommend, and with the memory of his own sojourn at St. Georges-d'Espéranche in mind, the king should have turned to Savoy for the expert direction and deployment of so widely drawn a labour force. That Savoy may not have been entirely the loser, that some who came returned, is suggested not only by the plan of Champvent, which is likely to reflect that of Conway rather than vice-versa, but also by the extraordinarily close resemblance of the early fourteenth-century east end of the church of St. Etienne at Moudon to the west front of Valle Crucis abbey (repaired after war damage in 1282–3) (Plate XLIc and d).[7] No easy explanation can be offered, but the suggestion of a direct connection seems inescapable. There are

---

[1] PRO, E101/351/9, m. 11; 351/12; *Archaeologia*, xvii. 306–7.

[2] Arthur Jones (ed.), 'Flintshire Ministers' Accounts, 1301–28', *Pubs. Flints. Hist. Soc.* 3 (Prestatyn, 1913), 95–6.

[3] *Hist. King's Wks.* ii. 716

[4] Ibid. i. 372 n. 2.

[5] *Bull. Bd. of Celtic Studies*, xxvii (1977), 254, quoting PRO, C47/3/21(11).

[6] *Proc. Brit. Acad.* xxxii. 17; diagrams showing their numbers and catchment areas are in Taylor, 'The Prelude to Construction' pp. 107, 111.

[7] For the history of Moudon see Charles Gilliard, *Moudon sous le Régime savoyard* (Méms. et Docts. publ. par la Soc. d'histoire de la Suisse romande, sér. 2, tome XIV); for St. Étienne, see Gaëtan Cassina, 'Saint-Étienne de Moudon' in series *Guides des Monuments Suisses*.

many unknowns in the story traced in the foregoing pages, and their solution may safely be left to the future.

Acknowledgements. I am indebted for permission to reproduce illustrations as follows: Crown Copyright reserved, Department of the Environment: Plates XXIII*a* and *b*, XXIV*a* and *d*, XXVI*a* and *b*, XXVII*a* and *b*, XXIX*a* and *c*, XXXII *a* and *c*, XXXIII*c*, XXXV*b* and *c*, XXXVIII*b*, XL*a*; Crown Copyright reserved, Public Record Office, Plate XLII*b* and *c*; Royal Commission on Ancient and Historical Monuments in Wales, Plate XL*b*; Max F. Chiffelle, Lausanne, Plate XXXIII*b*; J. Cellard, Lyon, Plate XXXIX*c*; Musée d'Art et d'Histoire, Genève, Plate XLI*a*, figs. 2 and 3; F. Rouge and Cie S. A. Lausanne, fig. 4; Society of Antiquaries of London, Plate XLI*b*; Archivio di Stato, Torino, fig. 1; Archs. Dept. de la Savoie, Chambéry, Plate XLII*a*.

¹ Besides debts of thanks acknowledged in the text or in previous footnotes, I gratefully recall help given me by MM. R. Avezou and Jean Sablou, and M. Sablou's successor M. Perret, Archivistes en chef of the Archives de l'Isère and de la Savoie at Grenoble and Chambéry respectively in the 1950s; by the late Baronne Elisabeth de Blonay at Grandson; by the late M. Hugues and Mme Jéquier at La Lance; and by M. Péclard at Champvent. I also have to thank Professor Marcel Grandjean for help in regard to the cathedral of Lausanne, and M. Gaëtan Cassina for help in regard to St. Etienne de Moudon. I am also infinitely indebted to M. Jean-Pierre Chapuisat for constant help and advice and companionship over a period of twenty years on visits to castles and churches in all parts of medieval Savoy, and to Jeanne and Lionel Stones for help during the preparation of this paper. The reconstruction drawing of Harlech (Plate XXXII) was kindly made by Mr. David Neal, and the redrawing of the 1794 plan of St. Georges by Mr. Frank Gardner, both of the Ancient Monuments Illustrators Branch of the Department of the Environment.

PLATE XXIII

a

b

Inclined scaffold lines on curtain walls

a. Conway   *b*. Beaumaris

PLATE XXIV

a

b

c

d

Helicoidal scaffold lines

a. Conway, Watch Tower   *b*. Conway, Upper Gate

c. Harlech, Gatehouse   *d*. Beaumaris, North Gatehouse

PLATE XXV

a

b

c

d

e

Helicoidal scaffold lines

a. and *b.* Saxon (Valais)

c. Harlech, SW tower   *d.* Conway, Prison tower   *e.* Saillon (Valais)

PLATE XXVI

a

b

Full-centred semi-circular arches

a. Conway Castle, E window of hall

b. Harlech Castle, window embrasures in SE tower

PLATE XXVII

a

b

Full-centred semi-circular arches

a. Beaumaris Castle, barbican

b. Harlech Castle, arch in S tower of gatehouse

PLATE XXVIII

a

b

c

d

Full-centred semi-circular arches

a. and *b.* Saillon (Valais), Porte du Sex   *c.* and *d.* Harlech, outer gateway

PLATE XXIX

a

b

c

d

Full-centred semi-circular arches

a. Harlech Castle, embrasure in NE tower
b. St. Georges-d'Espéranche, embrasure in SE tower
c. Conway Castle, embrasure in King's tower
d. Harlech Castle, door-head in gatehouse

PLATE XXX

Garderobe construction

a. Harlech Castle, NW tower   *b.* St. Georges-d'Espéranche (Isère), SE tower

c. Harlech, above S ditch   *d.* La Bâtiaz (Valais), NW curtain

PLATE XXXI

a

b

c

d

Triple finials on battlements

a. and *b.* Conway Castle, western towers

c. and *d.* S. Giorio in Val di Susa, crenellation of (?)*c.* 1300

PLATE XXXII

a

b

c

d

Harlech gatehouse windows

a. Gatehouse from W   *b*. Gatehouse, restoration drawing by David Neal

c. S window, restoration drawing by the late Leonard Monroe   *d*. S window

PLATE XXXIII

a

b

c

d

Harlech and Chillon windows

a. Chillon, view from lake   *b*. Chillon, window to courtyard (ext.)

c. Harlech, window to courtyard (int.)   *d*. Chillon, window to courtyard (int.)

PLATE XXXIV

a

b

c

a. Chillon from SE

b. Lausanne Cathedral, tomb of
Sir Otto de Grandison

c. Château de Grandson

PLATE XXXV

a

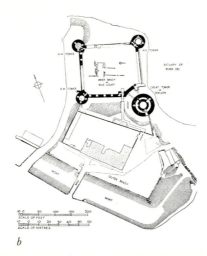

b

c

a. Château d'Yverdon (begun 1261), air view

b. Flint Castle (begun 1277), plan

c. Flint Castle, air view

PLATE XXXVI

a

b

a. Château de Champvent (Vaud), general view

b. Conway Castle, N façade

PLATE XXXVII

a

b

c

a. Château de Saillon (Valais), general view

b. Conway Town Walls and Castle from Bangor Road, by
Moses Griffith, 1806

c. Conway Town Walls, view from W

PLATE XXXVIII

a

b

c

a. Château de Saillon (Valais), curtain wall and flanking tower

b. Conway, Town Walls with flanking tower

c. Saxon (Valais), original putlog and remains of surface rendering

PLATE XXXIX

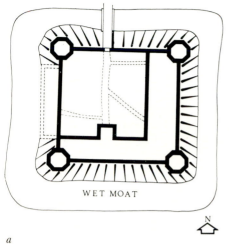

WET MOAT

N

a

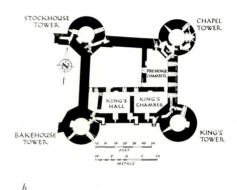

STOCKHOUSE
TOWER

CHAPEL
TOWER

N

PRESENCE
CHAMBER

KING'S
HALL

KING'S
CHAMBER

BAKEHOUSE
TOWER

KING'S
TOWER

FEET

METRES

b

c

a. St. Georges-d'Espéranche, plan based on drawing of 1794

b. Conway Castle, 1st-floor plan of inner ward

c. St. Georges, air view from E, with castle in left foreground

PLATE XL

a

b

c

d

e

Caernarvon and Constantinople

a. Caernarvon Castle from SW *b*. Caernarvon Castle, Queen's tower

c. and *d*. Constantinople, Theodosian Walls

e. Caernarvon, W wall of town, showing Porth-yr-aur or Golden Gate
(named as 'Gildyn yeate' in 1524)

PLATE XLI

a *b*

c *d*

a. Lausanne Cathedral, W window before restoration (drawing of 1902, from Marcel Grandjean, 'Chronologie et Maîtres d'Oeuvre de la Cathédrale', *Geneva* NS XI (1963), 261–87)

b. Conway Castle, E window of hall, reconstruction drawing by Sidney Toy, *Archaeologia* LXXXVI (1937), 186

c. Valle Crucis Abbey, Denbs., showing W gable as rebuilt after 1284

d. St. Etienne, Moudon (Fribourg), E end (first quarter of fourteenth century).

PLATE XLII

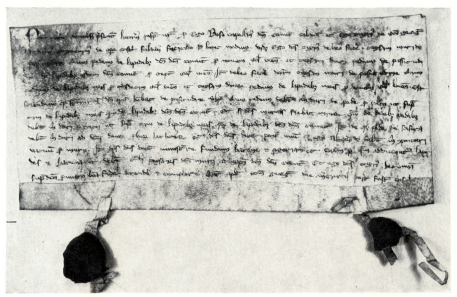

a. Contract between Count of Savoy's chaplain and Tassin of St. George, mason, for building works at Falavier (Isère), St. Georges, Wed. after Easter 1278 (Archs. de la Savoie, Chambéry, Inv. 135, fo.17. pqt.14, no.7)

b. Cancelled payment to Master Giles of St. George at Aberystwyth, Aug.–Sept. 1282 (PRO, C47/2/4)

c. Payments to transport contractors, including 'Gilet' and Adam Boynard, Harlech, March 1286 (PRO, E101/485/27)